JACQUELINE SUTHREN HIRST

SITA'S *story*

A PROJECT OF THE

DHARAM HINDUJA INSTITUTE

OF INDIC RESEARCH

FACULTY OF DIVINITY

UNIVERSITY OF CAMBRIDGE

HINDU
VALUES
SERIES

1

SERIES EDITOR: JULIUS LIPNER
Faculty of Divinity, University of Cambridge

RMEP

RELIGIOUS AND MORAL EDUCATION PRESS

Religious and Moral Education Press
An imprint of Chansitor Publications Ltd,
a wholly owned subsidiary of Hymns Ancient & Modern Ltd
St Mary's Works, St Mary's Plain
Norwich, Norfolk NR3 3BH

First published by Bayeux Arts Incorporated,
119 Stratton Cres. S.W., Calgary, Alberta, Canada 1997

First published in Great Britain by RMEP 1997

ISBN 1 85175 143 2

This edition is not available for sale in Canada and the U.S.A.

The Publishers gratefully acknowledge the generous support of the
Alberta Foundation for the Arts

Design: Carbon Media

Printed in Hong Kong by King's Time Printing
for Chansitor Publications Ltd., Norwich

Contents

Editor's Preface

The Dharam Hinduja Institute of Indic Research was established in the Divinity Faculty, University of Cambridge, in January 1995. Its aim is to study the major religious traditions based in India, with a special emphasis on Hinduism, in a way that contributes to the wellbeing of society. As part of an ongoing programme to reach out to different groups, this book is the first in the Hindu Values Series, written by experts in the field and sensitive to the needs of its readers. For some other titles in the series, see the back of this book.

There is an almost desperate need for good, easily readable books on the religious traditions in India. This need is all the greater in the west where many from the Indian sub-continent have settled, often cut off from their roots. It is important, therefore, to produce challenging texts, from an unsectarian point of view, by means of which western readers can have an unbiased account of the religious traditions in India, and South Asians learn more about their roots. Though the Series is aimed directly at young people, we hope that it will be of benefit to many others too — teachers, South Asian community groups, social workers and so on. If you've found it useful, please spread the word to as many as you think might benefit from it.

The author of this book, Dr Jacqueline Suthren Hirst, is ideally equipped to start off the Series. After completing an outstanding doctoral degree in Indian religion in the Divinity Faculty at Cambridge, she taught for a number of years at Homerton College, Cambridge University's teacher training college. She is now Lecturer in Comparative Religion at the University of Manchester. She has a deep knowledge and wide experience of her subject. Sita, the subject of this book, is also an excellent choice. Sita's story can help us understand not only the way stories are told about and by people and what we can learn from this, but also changing Hindu values and ideals, and how an appreciation of these can help all of us, Hindus and non-Hindus alike, live more interesting and fruitful lives.

Dr. Julius Lipner, Director,
Dharam Hinduja Institute of Indic Research
Faculty of Divinity, University of Cambridge
April 1997

Author's Preface

It would not have been possible to write this book without the help of those who kindly gave up their time to be interviewed about Sita's importance to them. For their generosity, openness and readiness to share an aspect of their lives, I thank: Manjusha Acharya, Maluika Acharya, Shakuben Jayanti Buhecha, Geeta Pandey, Shivani Pandey, Kanchan Lalji Pankhania, Bharat Pankhania, Krishna Kumari Pankhania, Vanita Popat, Dipen Popat, Tina Shah, Rajni Shah, Shilpa Shah, Trishna Shah, Jilna Shah and others who chose not to be named.

I hope that their very different voices will be heard through this book, as they reflect on the values which Sita expresses for them. As they do so, they continue the age-old human and Hindu custom of re-telling a crucial story and making its meanings their own. Their reflections are given in italic type, so that it is clear where those interviewed are speaking and where I am providing a framework for their views. The book is divided into sections which were shaped by the interviews. Under each section heading is a question to provoke your reflection as you read, whatever your own background may be. A further note for teachers is given at the back of the book. For the framework and questions, I alone am responsible, but I hope they will at least do justice to the diversity and thoughtfulness of those whose contributions really make Sita's story live.

A NOTE ON NAMES AND TERMS

In the book, the names of the characters in the story appear in two forms, e.g. **Rama/Ram**, Shiva/Shiv. The longer spelling is used in Sanskrit, the ancient classical language of India. Some modern Indian languages, like Hindi, prefer the shorter spelling. I have used both, depending on the context. The Glossary and List of Names at the back of the book give lists of important words and names in various Indian languages. The first time such a word is used in the text, it appears in **bold** type.

J. G. Suthren Hirst
March 1997

SITA'S *story*

It is a November evening in a darkened school hall. At one end, shadowy figures move behind a backlit screen. The audience waits in suspense as **Sita** sends **Rama** off to find the beautiful golden deer she has seen in the forest. A blood-curdling cry is heard. Sending **Lakshmana**, Rama's half-brother, to find out what the matter is, Sita is left alone. Enter **Ravana**, the ten-headed demon king of Lanka, disguised as a wandering holy man. Sita steps forward over the protective circle Lakshmana has drawn round her hut to offer the holy man food. In an instant, Ravana reveals his true form and Sita is kidnapped. Ravana carries her off in his chariot through the skies to his island palace of Lanka. The ancient story of Rama and Sita is being told in shadow puppet form.

The people who have made the puppets and are operating them are some of the school-age members of the **Gujarat**i Hindu community in Cambridge, England. The audience watching is engrossed, not just as proud parents and other elders, but because this story is part of their cultural heritage and the great Autumn festivals of **Navratri** and **Divali**. In this book, we shall try to explore why this story, and especially Sita's part in it, remains so important to Hindus and others across the world. Partly this seems to be because it is a story which raises issues which affect all human beings, things like:

> personal and social relationships,
> where we get our religious and cultural values,
> how we can understand others,
> the nature of stories,
> the power of the media,
> domestic violence and rape.

It is not for nothing that recent long-running Indian television serials of this story, The **Ramayana**, and the other great Indian epic, The *Mahabharata*, have been called 'Hindu soaps'!

Left: Sita Devi, a Malay shadow puppet.

The Spread of the Story

In India, the roots of this story go back, perhaps nearly three thousand years. It has been told countless times, by Hindus, Jains and Buddhists, and early spread beyond India itself to the countries of Southeast Asia. Today, if you visit the Grand Palace in Bangkok, Thailand, you can see beautiful carvings around the walls, telling a Thai Buddhist version of the story. In villages in Indonesia, professional puppeteers and musicians still present the story through shadow puppets or ordinary puppets, accompanied by the haunting music of the **gamelan**.

One of the oldest Hindu versions of the story is the **Sanskrit** poem by Valmiki, a poem which may have been revised and added to, as the story was constantly retold. Its core goes back to perhaps the fifth or fourth century BCE. Valmiki's *Ramayana* is often taken for granted in later retellings, though they may be different in important ways. One of the best-known of these is Tulsidas's sixteenth century *Ramcharitmanas*, told in **Hindi**. Tulsidas's story is very well-known throughout North India. It is the basis for the famous *Ram-lila* performances, which are held around the **Dassehra** festival in September or October. For Tulsidas, Rama and Sita are not just human figures. They are the divine on earth. In the *Ram-lilas*, actors from special families play the key roles, creating an atmosphere in which they 'become' Rama and Sita for the audience, embodying the divine in their midst.

Tulsidas's words were also used by Ramanand Sagar in his block-busting TV production. For 45 minutes each Sunday from January 1987 to July 1988, one hundred million Indians, of many different religious allegiances or none, would tune in to watch a serial which had to be extended three times by popular demand. It is now available on video and is watched avidly across the world, an international viewing record! Later in the book, this version will be discussed by some of the people interviewed. Their opinions were not all the same. . . . But first we must ask, is this really Sita's story?

Left: Scene from the Thai Ramayana, Grand Palace, Bangkok, Thailand.

Whose Story?

Can you be an individual, without relating to other people?

"How can you write a book about Sita without writing it about Ram as well?" I was asked by one person interviewed. It was a good question. Sita's story is inseparably linked with the story of her husband, Ram (or, Rama) and, indeed, with his wider family and the people of his kingdom, **Ayodhya**. This is very clear in Hindu shrines. Sita almost never stands alone. Rather, she stands on Rama's left and Lakshmana, Rama's half-brother, on his right. Hanuman, the monkey god, kneels in devoted service at their feet. Almost all the devotional pictures and photos of shrines you will see in this book follow a similar pattern, though Rama's other brothers and attendants may add to the group. This should warn us not to see Sita simply as an individual, but in relation to other people.

Should we then single out her story at all? Certainly, in some versions of the story, Sita is not even very prominent. "She seems rather a passive person," commented one teenager, "not active at all." But this does not apply to all tellings. Both men and women have written stories and sung songs where Sita has been a key character: the one around whom the story revolves, strong in herself, a vehicle for reflecting on their own experience. We shall see examples later in the book, but for now we need to turn to the story.

At right, from left to right: Lakshman, Ram, Sita, Hanuman kneeling.
'I reverence the feet of Sita and Rama, who though stated to be different, are yet identical just like a word and its meaning or like water and the waves on its surface, and to whom the afflicted are most dear' *(Tulsidas, 1.18)*

Sita's Story Told

What sort of character does Sita seem to be from this story?

As we have seen, there is no single version of Sita's story, but there is a common core of events which appear in most retellings. The story below is based on Tulsidas's *Lake of the Exploits of Rama*, but concludes with the very different ending from Valmiki's earlier poem.

King **Dashrath**, the king of Ayodhya, dearly longed for children. After he had performed a special ritual, four sons were born to his three wives. Ram was the eldest. The others were called Bharat, Lakshman and **Shatrughna**. Their human bodies were a form of Lord **Vishnu**, which he took to help overcome the demons who were oppressing the earth. As young men, Ram and Lakshman went with the great sage, Vishvamitra, to help him in this task. They finally came to **Mithila**, the capital city of King **Janak**, who was looking for a suitable husband for his beautiful daughter, Sita.

Sita herself had an unusual origin. She had been found by Janak one day, lying in a field which he was ploughing for a sacrifice. Her name means 'furrow' and she was a true daughter of the Earth, though adopted by the king. Women's songs from Andhra Pradesh tell how, as a young girl, she realised that her father had once left behind a family treasure, the great bow of Lord **Shiv**, so she picked it up and brought it to him. Other stories tell how she used to push it aside as she was performing household duties. Janak was truly amazed, because the bow was so heavy that no ordinary man could even move it. He realised that only a man who could pick it up would be worthy to marry his daughter.

As the women of Mithila watch Ram go round the town, with Lakshman and Vishvamitra, they gossip amongst themselves.

Left: Dasmukha and Sita, Javanese shadow puppets of Ravan and Sita.

"Here is a bridegroom worthy of Princess **Janaki**, king Janak's daughter, Sita."

"Will he be able to bend the bow?"

"Without a doubt. The same Creator, who made Sita with great skill, has preordained for her this dark-complexioned bridegroom."

At this point, Sita comes into the garden where Ram and Lakshman are gathering flowers for worship. A friend tells her of the princes and she is filled with an intense longing. 'No-one knew,' says the poet Tulsidas, 'that hers was an old love.' For Sita is none other than Ram's true consort, his eternal 'other half'. She goes to the temple of **Parvati** (Lord Shiv's wife) to pray for a suitable husband and the goddess promises her that her heart's desire will be fulfilled.

The next day is her *svayamvar*, the day she will choose as her husband the one who can move the bow. Suspense grows as none of the kings who has come is able to budge it an inch. Finally, Ram, with Vishvamitra's permission, steps forward. To Sita's mother, he seems a mere boy. What hope is there that he will succeed when others have failed? Will the family be a laughing-stock? Sita prays, agitated within, but calm without, and Ram not only picks up, but strings and breaks the bow! Modestly, Sita garlands her future husband and 'the pair shone as if beauty and love met together in human form'.

A splendid marriage follows, tinged with the usual sadness of an Indian girl's family saying goodbye to their precious daughter. It is matched, though, by the joy of the citizens of Ayodhya as they welcome home Ram and Sita, along with his other brothers and their wives, who also married in Mithila.

This happiness is soon marred, however. Dashrath wants to give the throne over to Ram, but **Kaikeyi**, the mother of Bharat, wants her son to be king. Calling on an old promise, she asks not only for this, but that Ram should be banished to the forest for fourteen years. Dashrath is heartbroken, but Ram is ready to obey, though he tries to persuade Sita to stay in Ayodhya without him. He stresses that she is delicate, lovely, timid and not at all fit for forest life. Sita is, however, clear: "There is no calamity in this world as great as being away from one's beloved lord." In other versions, she is even more adamant. With Lakshman,

Right: Bride and groom garlanded .

who leaves his wife **Urmila** behind, she goes with Ram into exile. Tulsidas sees her as the cosmic energy which comes between the individual soul (Lakshman) and God (Ram). The individual soul may be deluded by that Maya or it may be led by Maya to understand its true relation to God.

Meanwhile, Bharat, who was away from home while his mother was plotting, has returned to Ayodhya and is horrified to hear of Ram's exile. With the court, he goes to plead for their return or, at least, that of Sita. When they refuse, Bharat goes back to Ayodhya with a pair of Ram's sandals which he places on the throne until Ram rightfully returns.

Life in the forest is becoming dangerous. **Shurpanakha**, the sister of the demon king of Lanka, sees Ram, is passionately attracted to him and tries to seduce him. Glancing at Sita, Ram suggests Shurpanakha try Lakshman — a bachelor, he teases. (He's not, Urmila is back in Ayodhya.) Sita is now terrified. Ram signals to Lakshman who cuts off the demoness's nose and ears. Mutilated and enraged, she goes to her brother, Ravan, for revenge. Ram, realising danger, urges Sita to enter into a special fire which will protect her till he has completed the destruction of the demons. Ever loyal, she does as he bids, leaving him with only her shadow, which looks and behaves just as the real Sita does and fools even Lakshman. Then it happens that Ravan, disguised as a holy man, approaches Sita's forest hut. Earlier, Sita has seen a golden deer (a demon in disguise) and sent Ram off to fetch it for her. Lakshman has followed, at Sita's insistence, when a terrible scream is heard. Taking for granted the well-known story that Lakshman drew a circle round the hut before leaving, Tulsidas tells us of Ravan's approach, alternately wooing and threatening Sita. Though terrified, Sita plucks up her courage and compares him with a tiny hare who would marry a lioness. "So have you wooed your own destruction!" she warns. Nothing daunted, Ravan kidnaps her, whisking her through the air in his chariot.

Ram, returning, is distressed like an ordinary person and mournfully thinks about her. "O Sita, Janak's daughter, the very mine of virtues, of such flawless beauty, character, austerity and devotion!" We then lose sight of this virtuous Sita while Ram and Lakshman help a dispossessed monkey king, Sugriva, and in return gain the services of the monkeys and other animals in searching for Sita. In the end, it is the monkey Hanuman, son of the wind, who

Left: Sita sees the golden deer, from *Ramayanas* as told by *Valmiki* and *Kamban*.

leaps across the sea to the island fortress of Lanka, takes Ram's ring to Sita and gives her Ram's message telling of his agony of separation from her. First Hanuman sees Ravan trying to win Sita over. Sita is emaciated, thin in her sorrow, her hair in a single plait because separated from her husband. Yet she remains determined. "Perhaps you have no idea what Shree Ram's arrow shafts are like, O wretch!" Inside, though, she is grief-stricken and doubts whether Ram ever remembers her. Hanuman's assurance and stories of Ram renew her strength and she agrees to wait patiently, sending Hanuman back to Ram with her blessings.

A terrible battle for Lanka then takes place. In Valmiki's version, Ravan taunts Sita with a lie about Ram's death and a fictitious head of Ram which he creates. However, one of her demoness guards, Trijata, a good character, particularly in Tulsidas, assures her that Ram will kill Ravan, once Ravan forgets Sita in his heart. At last, Hanuman comes to Sita with the message of Ram's success. 'Her soul was overjoyed, a thrill ran through her body and with eyes full of tears **Rama** said again and again, "What can I give you? There is nothing in all the three worlds equal in value to this information."' By calling Sita 'Rama', Tulsidas emphasises how she really belongs with Ram.

Meanwhile, Ram arranges for a special carriage to be sent to fetch Sita. Bathed and beautifully dressed, Sita gets into the palanquin to return to Ram, her husband, her thoughts completely fixed on him 'the all-blissful one, her loving lord'. Then Tulsidas reminds his listeners that, up to now, it has been the **shadow Sita** who has undergone all these sufferings. When this Sita reaches Ram, he addresses her reproachfully, we are told. This remark only makes sense if we know Valmiki's version or others where the returning real Sita is met, not with a joyful reunion, but spurned, accused of having been unfaithful to Ram while with Ravan.

So accused, Sita commands Lakshman to make her a fire and calls on the fire to become cold, providing she has never set her heart on anyone other than Ram, in thought, word or deed. Entering the flames, she remains unscathed. In Valmiki's version, Ram is delighted. Though he never really doubted Sita himself, her purity has now been demonstrated to all the people who might otherwise have suspected her fidelity and lost confidence in Ram if he had received an unfaithful woman back. Tulsidas comments that both the shadow Sita

Right: Ravan abducts Sita, from a popular Amar Chitra Katha comic.

(who is unknown to Valmiki) and the social stigma of having been with Ravan were consumed by the fire. It is the real and ever pure Sita who emerges.

The way is paved in Tulsidas for the joyful return of Ram, Sita and Lakshman to Ayodhya, where Sita's first act is to greet her mothers-in-law, including the scheming Kaikeyi, with happy devotion. The women bathe and bejewel her and the whole land rejoices that Ram and Sita are once more together and on the throne. Sita performs her household tasks, waits on her mothers-in-law and, in passing, it is mentioned that she has twin sons, **Kush** and **Lav**. There Tulsidas leaves Sita's story, finishing his poem with accounts of the way the story has been passed on since that time. 'This glorious, holy, purifying, blessed and clear Lake of Ram's Exploits always brings happiness; it gives wisdom and devotion, wipes out **delusion**, infatuation and impurity and is brimming over with the water of love.' Through devotion to Ram's Name and seeing Ram and Sita in all the world, people will be freed from the endless world of rebirth.

Valmiki and others don't go for such a happy ending, at least in the full-length version we have today. After Ram and Sita have been crowned, rumours of Sita's unfaithfulness start up again. In one version, Ram overhears a low-caste washerman saying that he would not even have his wife back after she'd spent a night out on the other side of the river because there was no-one to bring her back, yet King Ram was willing to have Sita back, though she'd been in Ravan's company all that long time. Ram banishes Sita from Ayodhya, even though she is now pregnant, because it is more important for him as king to uphold the social order than to consider his own feelings as husband or Sita's as his wife. When Ram first discovered Sita was expecting, he asked what she would like. She wanted to visit the sages in the forest. So now, under pretext of fulfilling this wish, he asks Lakshman to take Sita beyond the borders of the kingdom. Lakshman does so but is filled with grief. Sita despairs, then charges Lakshman to return and declare her purity to Ram: "You should have spared me, since you are my only refuge." The sage Valmiki, composer of the poem himself, leaves Sita in the care of some female renouncers. When Kush and Lav are born, it is Valmiki who tells them the story of Ram and Sita and commands them to recite the Ramayana.

Years later, Ram hears one such recitation, recognises his sons and sends a message to Sita

Left: Sita's fire ordeal which proves her innocence.

that, if she is without sin and wants to prove it, she can come to the court and do so. Sita comes sobbing, her mind still intent on Ram. Valmiki swears her innocence. Sita now, though, calls on the Earth Goddess, her Mother, to receive her, "If, in thought, I have never dwelt on any but Rama." From the earth a throne appears, blossoms fall from the sky, Sita descends into the earth and a tremor is felt. Ram is now distraught. Though he continues to rule for an exceedingly long reign, with a golden image of Sita by his side, he never really recovers and, in the end, gives up his throne, banishes Lakshman and succumbs to death, followed by his loyal subjects, human and animal.

So whose story is it, in the end?

Just as Sita's story has been handed down in many different written and spoken forms, so the way it was told me by those interviewed varied considerably, in depth and detail. Key episodes which were mentioned by most people included: Sita's *svayamvar*, seen as her own choice of husband; her exile into the forest with Ram and Lakshman; her devotion to Ram during that time and her faithfulness when taken by Ravan to Lanka; the fire test on her return; the crowning of Ram and Sita in Ayodhya. *"I'd leave it here, it's the main bit most people know about,"* said one university student, true to Tulsidas' ending. Others reported the rumours. *"These children are not from Ram. Sita was kidnapped by Ravan. Maybe they are his."* Two commented on the tragedy of Lakshman taking Sita into exile yet again. More completed the story with Sita being swallowed up by the Earth.

Most people were not aware of the 'shadow Sita' theme. The women who did know it read Tulsidas regularly, as part of their own devotions. Tulsidas borrowed this from an earlier version, the *Adhyatma-ramayana*. It is a device which ensures that the real Sita, who remains behind, is kept absolutely pure; it is not left up to Sita herself to maintain her purity while in Ravan's palace. It also softens Ram's harshness on her return, for the fire episode then becomes a way of restoring the real Sita and laying the rumours to rest, once and for all. There was no such softening in the minds of those who heard Sita's story as one of suffering by the real person. The version they knew and the ways in which they had learned it tended to affect the way they saw Sita and her impact, if any, on their own lives. So before we ask what sort of character Sita is, we shall stop to ask how it is that people know her story at all.

Right: Sita's mother earth receives her, from the exhibition at the Cultural Festival of India, London, 1985

Getting to Know the Stories

How have you learned about your own family and culture?

"How," I asked early in each interview, "did you get to know the stories about Sita?" *We learnt it from grandparents and parents too. If we didn't want to go to bed, in the evening, we would ask, "Tell us a story,"* replied one woman.

Another, who had also been brought up in East Africa, described such story-telling in her family: *In Africa, in Kenya, at night time, sitting near the fire. I was the eldest and had four brothers and three sisters. My grandmother made me sit and read Ramayan and got me to explain and my grandmother would listen and correct and explain too . . . Every day you read as much as you like. I still do this every evening. In Africa, we used to read at sunset. It was more fun when we were little. All the neighbour's children came and listened too.*

A similar experience was quite common amongst others interviewed who are now parents themselves, whether brought up in India or East Africa. Their children range from their twenties down to primary school age. For these children, other forms of entertainment have taken the place of readings round the fire as ways of learning about the story — *Amar Chitra Katha* comics (see picture on p.19) and especially the video versions from Indian television. Particularly popular is a four-cassette version, *Lavkush*. Like the first book of Valmiki's poem, it tells the Ramayan story in short form, as well as giving the longer ending with considerable pathos. It was often the source from which both younger and older generations drew their own account of the story.

For some, Sita and others on video are a tribute to the modern world. Their video popularity shows that the old stories still have relevance today. People are happy that the younger generation will continue to learn the old stories, even if they are living in a different culture which doesn't

Left: Mrs. Kanchan Pankhania reading her copy of Tulsidas's *Ramcharitmanas.* The small square cloth is a *gadi,* a 'throne' where Hanuman is invited in prayer to sit, before worshipful reading is begun.

really understand them. Others are less happy. They fear the other ways of learning the story may be brushed aside, that the many different versions of the story may be reduced to one, not altogether satisfactory, TV version. This raises a question which concerns us all about the power of the electronic media. Is the power of TV and video a good power, spreading understanding both of our own traditions and of other cultures, if we take time to let it? Or is it an arrogant power, taking too much upon itself, a modern Ravan with multiple heads, unable to listen to others?

Although there was some evidence of a uniformity in telling the story, many different ways of learning it and reacting to it seemed to be alive and well amongst those I interviewed. Two traditional methods in particular persist. One is getting to know more of the story in a very informal way, by questioning a mother or grandmother about details of the story, daily worship, festivals or household pictures. *We learnt by asking our own questions about the characters: who were they? whose daughter was Sita? who were their parents? and so on.*

When we pray we say 'Sita-Ram'. In **kirtan** *we sing, "Jay Shree (=Sita) Ram." It shows she's an important character. . . Perhaps women should come first, then men. . .and have respect because of Sita. As children, we would ask, "Why do we say Sita first?"*

We celebrate Divali in relation to when Ram and Sita came from exile. They told it to us as the story behind why we celebrate.

The other is by going to a *katha*, a public story-telling event in which the whole of the story, often the *Ramcharitmanas*, is recited over nine, ten or thirty days. A skilful story-teller adds explanations, additional stories, modern examples and jokes to keep both young and old entertained. One of the most famous Gujarati narrators is Morari Bapu. Many Hindus living in Europe or North America will take their annual holiday to coincide with his visit to their country — or make it a reason for going abroad to hear him. He is very popular with children and teenagers and speaks in English as well as Gujarati and Hindi. His *Mangal Ramayan* is full of anecdotes, drawing on a wide range of Sufi (Muslim) as well as Hindu sayings. Throughout, he stresses the importance of both Ram and Sita to worshippers today. So, if Sita's story, in a wide variety of forms, seems to go on being popular, this leads us to our next question: Why go on telling the story?

Above: Morari Bapu giving a *katha* in Canada recently

Facing page: Valli Subbiah dancing Sita asking, with her left hand, for the golden deer, shown by her right hand. Dance is another popular medium for passing on traditional stories.

Why go on Telling the Story?

What stories do you know which are true to your own experience?

---

*T*he people of my parent's generation, they believe that it's true, because of their upbringing. For them, it's a fact, a matter of history. To me, it's more like Chinese whispers. You get exaggeration in any story. The world's not like that really.

I can't really relate to it [the story of Sita and Ram]. As a story, it's just a small story in the history of literature. There's a lot more subsequent to that. I've never really thought about it, more than just being told about it.

These comments were made by two Hindu men in their twenties. At one level, in different ways, they were both prepared to dismiss the story. At another level, each was deeply committed to certain of the values which the story explores, in particular those to do with family relationships, respect and support. *The philosophy of the story is more important than whether there's a good version out on video,* said one. *If you agree with it and pass it on to your children, that's what's important.*

So a second question might be: is telling the story of Sita (and others) a good way for Hindu parents to pass on their values to their children? Alongside that, we might ask how we have received and shaped our own values? Some seemed to think the story was not a good way nowadays. Children might be inclined to dismiss it as 'just a story', particularly given the many gods, animals, demons and other characters who perform amazing feats, like flying through the air and using magical weapons. Far from showing life 'as it was', which seems important to many older Hindus, it might just bring the whole tradition into ridicule, especially in the eyes of outsiders.

Left: A small *mandir* for Sita-Ram in Shilpa's bedroom, at ease with British teen culture!

Others, though, think that a story is a better way than a lot of 'do this, don't do thats'. At a simple level, younger children can *learn to recognise different characters, the bad ones and their bad associations. And Ram and Sita as appropriate characters, with their minds filled with good and pure thoughts, examples of purity and strength.* As they grow older, they may start to appreciate parts of the story which did not make much sense to them before. Shilpa, aged 13, felt that, having watched the video many times and heard explanations, she now understands the story better. For her mother and others of the same generation, the character of Sita became important with adolescence and, later, approaching marriage. It was then that they were told, "Be like Sita", an example of devotion to her husband and in-laws alike. For them growing up, as for young Hindus now, the story could then become a source of questioning and discussion about relationships and values.

My daughter asked me about Kaikeyi, "Why didn't Dashrath divorce her?" [since he was so unhappy with the way she made him exile Ram]. *She also said, "Because Dashrath had four sons, he didn't have a clue about daughters. That's why they treated Sita so delicately, as so lovely, a special person. If Ram had had sisters, would they still treat wives like this?"* The daughter questions the portrait of Sita given in the story she has learned. Is it really appropriate for today, she asks, not just for Hindu women but for Hindu men? We shall look at other questions later. Here we note that the story gives her the possibility of questioning and discussing, not just rebelling against, her parents' values.

As we have seen, one of the stumbling blocks about the story for some of the younger people interviewed was that the world of gods, demons and miracles just doesn't seem to fit in with a modern scientific view of the world. For many Hindus, including some of the younger generation, it is important not to dismiss that other world. Miracles and the manifestation of the divine, especially in holy teachers, female and male, are part of today's world for them. Others, though, may just reject the whole story out of hand. Then the question arises: are its themes still ones we recognise today: love and longing for another person, rejection and fear of being forgotten, conflict between public and private duty, family ties and pleasures? Perhaps that's where a comment on the *Ram-lila* performances becomes important. Their style makes 'gods and demons, sages and kings, begin to sound like one's relatives and neighbours', says Philip Lutgendorf in *The Life of a Text*, p.335. Re-enter the Indian soap!

Right: *Ram-lila* crowns for Ram and Sita, now in the museum at Banaras Hindu University, India. King and queen, husband and wife, people like ones down the road?

"Be Like Sita"

Is there anyone you want to be like?

---

*E*ven in general conversation, we were told, "Try to be like Sita," volunteered one of my first interviewees, a mother in her late thirties. Others of her generation confirmed a similar experience, unprompted. *We were told to follow her. . .We were brought up to do fasting and prayers. We were told, "Sita used to do this."* For these women, Sita was offered - and gladly accepted - as a kind of example for them to follow in their own lives. This suggested to me that she was acting as some kind of role model. Almost everyone interviewed was uneasy with this idea, though. This seemed to be partly because of a sense that Sita was no ordinary woman, so the ideal she offers is somewhat beyond reach. *Yes, she is ideal, but it's not "Be like Sita." She's not a role model. I can't reach her. I'm just human. If they're saying, "Be like Sita," they just mean, "Obey your husband and be faithful to him."* She hinted that this was indeed a way of getting women to conform, but that this wasn't the real meaning of what it might be to follow Sita's ideal.

Even amongst those who had accepted Sita as an example for their own lives, there was general agreement that they would not, in turn, tell their daughters to be like Sita. Partly this was due to a very Hindu sense that what is appropriate for one is not necessarily appropriate for all. We each have our own **dharma** to follow. Still, others can learn from Sita's unself-centred behaviour: *Sita's not necessarily an example to other women. She did what was expected as Lord Ram's wife — what was right for her and in the eyes of God. . . not because she had to, but because she chose to. In a way we should follow what she did, but she didn't do it to be followed.* Partly, the older generation felt that it might be counter-productive to insist on their own values when living in a different culture: *No, I wouldn't have Sita as a role model for my daughter. Too many expectations. I am quite happy that she is Indianised. She behaved so well in India recently, going everywhere . . never made any fuss.* I asked what more it would mean to take Sita as a role model. *To be more religious, marrying according to my choice, to behave as I did — I don't think she will do that, but I*

Left: Ideals in stained glass? A beautiful window in the new Ram Mandir, Leicester, UK.

will expect her to respect her husband, be honest with her husband, have a one man, one woman relationship.

Mother of three daughters, Tina Shah explained: *It's unfair to say to them, "You should be like that." We can hardly say we are like Dashrath and* **Kaushalya.** *It's appropriate to ask them to follow guidelines though.*

This also indicates the third reason for reluctance to say, "Be like Sita." This was a sense of the difference between life as it really is now and the ideal of Sita's story. They would pass on the story and leave the next generation to make up their own minds. Kanchan Pankhania and Shakuben Buhecha agreed as they discussed this point:

K: *We've taught our daughters the story and introduced them to our tradition. We don't say, "Follow Sita's role or follow Madonna's role!"*

Sh: *To follow Sita, you need Ram! They can't be like Sita. All we say is, "Try to act as reasonably as possible. Don't be outrageous."*

K: *Yes. Boys are looking for a girl like Sita: beautiful-looking, good as a housewife and mother. Today's generation says, "Are you a Rama?"*

A little later, I asked Bharat and Krishna, Pankhania brother and sister in their twenties, about being like Sita. They had not overheard their mother's conversation.

Krishna Kumari (the sister): *I can't relate to it* [being like Sita]. *She's too simple and straightforward, too obedient. I'm not like that at all. I make too many demands!*

Bharat: *If you find one* [a girl like Sita], *I'll marry her! It's relatively easy to make a traditional woman more Western, hard to make a Western girl more traditional. Such a girl would be homely, a good wife, good mother, have religious values, practise . . .* He mentioned weddings, **puja** and dress sense as things that would be affected. Krishna agreed that she'd know what to do and when, but then added: *You can't train a woman. She's not a pet!*

In her view, her brother was still taking Sita, or an ideal of womanhood expressed by Sita, as a role model in a rather unreformed way. Not that she rejected the values Sita has been held to show, like purity, faithfulness, self-denial and gentleness. *Every woman has some of these in her. Even a slight amount in me! I would want them — for respect for family and elders. But I'd want my husband to have the same for me.* No Sita without a modern-day Rama, as several of the older women indicated. How, then, is Sita seen?

The Ideal
Wife, Family Member
and Mother

What expectations do you have of your family, and your family of you?

Most of the interviewees automatically identified Sita as the dutiful wife, when asked what they would say about her. Below are three responses, one neutral in tone, one praising, one with a little edge:

The wife of Ram . . really devoted, didn't leave him, faithful when taken to Lanka . . but then most women in Hindu mythology are devoted to God and their husbands, willing to sacrifice themselves. It's the way women are meant to be (Female university student).

Sita followed in the footsteps of Ram. She agreed to do everything he said — it was the duty of a wife — to show the people that what her husband has done is the right thing. She gives an example to us. Both a husband and wife should go the same way — like two wheels of a chariot (Female Post Office owner).

Sita? Ram's wife. She chose to go into exile. She could have stayed in the palace, but she acted like a proper, devoted little wife (A second female university student).

As the second person indicates, this is not just a matter of Sita's relationship with Rama. They act as they do for the sake of the people. Rama's responsibility as king and Sita's as queen are more important than their own private feelings. *Because she is Rajrani* [Queen], *all her actions are in accordance with those expected by the subjects, irrespective of what she was suffering as a wife. It's a bit like Diana and Charles . . . They are not showing commitment to create a marriage. If you present the Queen* [of England] *with the states of her children's own marital affairs, she appears calm and collected. Who knows what she's going through? She can't show her anger and disagreement publicly.*

We all know what it is like to have expectations put upon us, to have to act differently in different situations. Sita is no different in this, says the story. We can identify with her.

As well as ideal wife, Sita is an ideal family member, especially in the way she relates to her mothers-in-law. *When I think of her, it's in a situation not just of a married couple but more of an extended family situation — how you possibly would be,* said a young girl in her twenties, with a marriage not yet organised. *She was so innocent, so sweet, she would do everything for the family. Thinking of it today, it's how I'd have to give respect, how she treated her in-laws and gave them respect.* There was no resentment in her voice.

This idea of respect and the family honour which goes with it is absolutely vital to many from a **South Asian** background, whether they are Hindu, Sikh or Muslim. It is such a fundamental cultural value that many of those interviewed felt that it was Sita who showed this kind of respect as a good Indian woman, rather than herself setting the original example to follow. For those who were told to be like Sita though, this respect for one's in-laws was a crucial part of what they were being taught.

For many women in India, the early experience of going to live with their husband's family after marriage has not been easy in the past. There were different customs to follow and more senior women, especially their mother-in-law, whose authority had to be accepted. Their husband was not their own. Sita's devoted example is given as a way of smoothing things over, showing that mutual appreciation and happiness can indeed develop, bad patches can be got through. Sitting by the millstone in Gujarat or **Maharashtra**, peasant women compare the suffering of Sita's exile with their own life under their in-laws:

> Sita has left for the forest; wild cows cross her path.
> This harsh lot of a daughter-in-law is all because of that beastly Ravana. . .
> To Sita, the harsh lot of a daughter-in-law brought troubles as numerous as the hairs
> on one's head.

Left: Current wedding ideals, superimposed on a page from a book telling Sita and Ram's story, photographed by 'Kaushik'.

She sent a share of it to her sisters, country after country.
To Sita, the harsh lot of a daughter-in-law came a grain at a time.
She sent a share of it to her relatives, village after village
(quoted in Poitevin and Rairkar, *Indian Peasant Women Speak Up*, p.67).

The song gives them solidarity with Sita, a way of coping with their own situations. How many songs in the charts work because the person listening identifies with the singers' feelings or situation, with their relationships or rejection? Common human themes, though contexts vary greatly. And it must be remembered that many Hindus outside India choose to maintain extended family networks, because they offer all kinds of financial, practical and emotional support that Western nuclear families often lack. Does the ideal family exist? Can there be a true Sita without a true Rama?

Finally, Sita can be seen as the ideal mother, both in her loyalty to Rama and the way she brought up her twin sons in the forest.

Sita never poisoned Lav and Kush against Ram. She showed no selfishness in this situation. . . She brought them up as ordinary children, to make do for themselves. She was down to earth, teaching them the basics. She could have made them 'little princes', but she didn't.

Still, when Sita appeals to the earth to swallow her, *You feel sorry for the children*, said a teenager. She understood that Sita knew what she had to do, but could sympathise with her sons, now missing their key parent. Sita's story is no more easy than life for many of us today.

Sita's Qualities

What qualities would you look for in a partner?

One recent Indian male writer, Sudhir Kakar, has said that Sita's main qualities are: purity, faithfulness in the face of rejection, willingness for self-sacrifice and gentle tenderness. He suggests that these are qualities which make women repress their own wishes and conform to what men want instead. *At the end of the day*, confirmed a 21 year old, *Asian men want the women to listen to them. They all say, "I want to marry an Indian girl."* Not so Shivani's 'non-religious' male cousin living in India. For him, Sita is too submissive an ideal. Do the other ideas expressed below bear out Kakar's view? Early in each interview, I asked what values or qualities Sita showed. Time and again, her loyalty, faithfulness and willingness to put others first came up, as in Kakar's list. They were linked with others clearly seen in a very positive light as the values which make life work.

She was kind, loved everyone. She even bowed down to Kaikeyi. She could forgive and forget, said one teenager. Later, she struggled with this a bit. *It's not really realistic. Kaikeyi was so selfish . .You'd think Sita would have some feelings against her . . .*

If you want to be part of a well-functioning body, function well yourself, said her mother separately. Some of the qualities she identified for Sita were: *pride that Rama had faith she would survive* [when he sent her into the forest], *patience, enduring hardship — she didn't complain.*

Later, I asked the interviewees to comment specially on the four qualities Kakar picked out. There was almost unanimous agreement that these qualities were positive, but could be abused.
Are these good values? For whom? For Sita? For me? For Hindu society? For Sita, yes, because in this way she expressed herself as an ideal princess, queen, mother, wife, all the way. For Hindu society - if you use them in the proper way, yes. I mean, if they don't take advantage of this kind of thing. Come to the present day. If somebody's polite, people shouldn't take advantage of their ideas if they are soft and gentle. Don't misuse that gentleness. Don't abuse their nature.

On Purity

How easy is it to say 'No' if you want to?

---

*T*here *is a* **chopai** *that Sita never looked towards Ravan because she was so loyal towards her husband. She didn't even want to see another man. It was when Ravan was asking her questions in prison in Lanka, trying to seduce her:*

'She picked a little grass, put it in front of her eyes like a curtain, then talked to him . . .'

तृन धरि ओट कहति बैदेही   trin dhari aut kahati baidehi . . .

Literally it means, 'Holding grass like a curtain, Sitaji says. . .'

Because she was so loyal, a one-man woman, she didn't even look at him. All of a sudden it came into my mind. It's really the best chopai to write for Sitaji. It shows her character, how strong she was. Give it to prove that we respect Sita very much.

Most of my peers at university would also accept these values, commented one student, a little unexpectedly. Another student remarked more sanguinely about purity and chastity, *You either believe it or you don't. I have a Roman Catholic friend who feels the same as I do. It should be taught to both sexes.* She implied that in India it was less important for boys, but that this shouldn't be the case. What do you think?

Right: The *Ramcharitmanas* open for reading. Red kumkum powder has been placed on the foreheads of Ram's brothers, Ram, Sita and Hanuman, as part of the purifying worship offered before reading.

श्रीरामपंचायतन

नीलांबुजश्यामळकोमळांग्ं सीतासमारोपितवामभागम् ।
पाणौ महासायकचारुचापं नमामि रामं रघुवंशनाथम् ॥

श्री रामचरितमानस

शुद्ध गुजराती भाषांतर

बालकाण्ड प्रारंभ

॥ मंगलाचरण ॥

श्लोकाः—वर्णानामर्थसंघानां रसानां छन्दसामपि ।
मङ्गलानां च कर्तारौ वन्दे वाणीविनायकौ ॥ १ ॥

अक्षरो, अर्थसमूहो, रसो, छंद तथा मंगळोना करनारी सरस्वती तथा गणपतिने हुं वंदन करुं छुं. १

भवानीशङ्करौ वन्दे श्रद्धाविश्वासरूपिणौ ।
याभ्यां विना न पश्यन्ति सिद्धाः स्वान्तःस्थमीश्वरम् ॥ २ ॥

श्रद्धा तथा विश्वासस्वरूप श्रीपार्वतीने तथा श्रीशंकरने हुं वंदन करुं छुं,
के जेमना विना सिद्ध लोको पोताना अंतःकरणमां रहेला ईश्वरने जोई
शकता नथी. २

वन्दे बोधमयं नित्यं गुरुं शङ्कररूपिणम् ।
यमाश्रितो हि वक्रोऽपि चन्द्रः सर्वत्र वन्द्यते ॥ ३ ॥

ज्ञानमय अने नित्य शंकररूप गुरुने हुं वंदन करुं छुं, जेमनो आश्रित
थयेलो वांको चंद्र पण जगत्‌मां सर्वत्र वंदाय छे. ३

सीताराम्गुणग्रामपुण्यारण्यविहारिणौ ।
वन्दे विशुद्धविज्ञानौ कवीश्वरकपीश्वरौ ॥ ४ ॥

श्रीसीताजी तथा श्रीरामचंद्रजीना गुणसमूहरूपी पवित्र वनमां विहार
करनारा अने विशुद्ध विज्ञानयुक्त कवीश्वर—श्रीवाल्मीकि तथा कपीश्वर—श्रीहनुमानजीने
हुं वंदन करुं छुं. ४

उद्भवस्थितिसंहारकारिणीं क्लेशहारिणीम् ।
सर्वश्रेयस्करीं सीतां नतोऽहं रामवल्लभाम् ॥ ५ ॥

उत्पत्ति, स्थिति (पालन) तथा संहार करनारां, क्लेशने हरनारां अने
संपूर्ण कल्याणोने करनारां श्रीरामना प्रियतमा श्रीसीताजीने हुं नमुं छुं. ५

On Faithfulness

What do partners have the right to expect of one another?

Almost all the people interviewed agreed on the ideal of one partner for life, perseverance when things go wrong in a relationship, the dangers of too easy divorce, though the younger people were not so set against the idea of divorce as their parents. Even some of the older women were prepared to criticise faithfulness if it really meant male domination.

It's ridiculous. Why do you have to follow whatever your husband's doing without knowing whether he's doing right or wrong? Yes, it's fine to follow your husband obediently if he acts rightly, but why should you, if he doesn't?

On Self-sacrifice

Have you had to make sacrifices for anyone? Who has made sacrifices for you?

Sita's self-sacrificial giving as queen, wife and mother is clearly an inspiration to many Hindu women in their own lives today.

Sita's sacrifices were made as queen for the kingdom. They are like us for our family. We are doing this for them.

A teenager starting to think about her own future relationships commented, *Self-denial can go too far. You can get trodden on. But Sita wasn't trodden on. She had self-respect and therefore she got respect. She held her head high and coped, even with Ravan.*

On Gentle Tenderness

Is this kind of sentimentality cultural play-acting or a real sign of strength?

This was rarely mentioned spontaneously, though one woman acknowledged, *That is how they describe her in the holy books.*

About to visit India for the first time in eight years, one student commented: *Indian gentleness is different. You are taught to be very feminine. To act. There are ways of talking to relatives and so on. It's really a different language. I wish I was better at it because it would be useful. I wouldn't feel so awkward. Female relatives expect me to be more girly. It's easier to talk to my uncles about politics.*

In a different light, another student said: *Gentle tenderness could be strong or weak .. depends on your viewpoint. But in order to be gentle and tender, you have to be strong to show it in caring for someone, don't you?*

Sita: Weak or Strong?

How would you identify true strength of character?

By and large, Sita was seen not as a weak character at all, but as one with great inner strength. The suggestion that she might be thought of as weak was frequently greeted with surprise. This does not mean she was beyond criticism, though, especially by the younger generation. *She doesn't stand up for herself enough. Why doesn't she speak back? She takes too much.*

Not all the older generation were unsympathetic either. *In our day it was, "Yes, sir, no, sir, three bags full, sir."* Her voice was sharp with remembrance. *Today they say, "Why should I? What for?" I say, "It helps sometimes. Do it for the sake of peace." She asks, "Why did Sita put up with all this? Nobody asked her to go [to the forest]."*

Speaking more gently, Maluika suggested: *She could have been more assertive when Ram questioned her [when she returned from Ravan]. She shouldn't have been so taken in by the beauty of the deer. She should have stopped to question what she saw.* Kamban, writing his **Tamil** story in the twelfth century, already agreed. Sita's ironic response to Rama's criticisms is nothing if not robust!

> All that I suffered,
> all the care
> with which I kept my chastity,
> my goodness,
> and at what cost,
> and for so long a time —

Left: The central shrine in the Ram Mandir, Leicester, UK. Sita appears gentle, devoted, yet strong.

all this seems crazy now,

a futile waste,

since you, O best of beings,

don't understand it in your heart

(translated by David Shulman in Paula Richman, p.103).

This reminds us sharply that different versions show Sita quite differently and that different people respond to a single version in many ways. Attitudes to Ramanand Sagar's TV version provide a good example of this. *When you saw the real thing*, remarked one young man, slightly off his guard, but echoing quite a widespread feeling that this version portrayed life as it really was. For Hindus who garlanded their TV sets and made offerings to Rama and Sita when they appeared it was 'the real thing' in an even stronger sense. Taking **darshan** is a key part of Hindu worship. It means to see God as present and be seen in turn. Just as the divine is seen as present in temple images and *Ram-lila* performances, so too it has been seen here on the TV screen. Viewers' own devotion to Sita-Ram has been strengthened in this way, Sita being seen as no other than Lord Ram's 'eternal other half', strength divine.

It's not then surprising that one of the interviewees who saw Sita in the TV version in this way was noticeably offended when I mentioned the following outspoken criticism from a female university student. However, it's important to realise that the student is not criticising Sita, but the 1988 TV's portrayal of her.

She's a bimbo figure, with loads of make-up and jewellery. Sita was a wonderful person. That shouldn't be confused with appearances. It's a glamorous programme, showing modern India's values which are different from the Ramayana. . . *The film's version of her is weak — done by some man! It just adds to stereotype images.* A weak portrayal of an essentially strong character and a dangerous one at that, she perhaps suggests. Two Indian feminists reviewing this version agreed, but went much further. We shall look at their comments in the next section but one, but first need to understand why so many do see Sita as essentially strong.

Right: A worshipper taking *darshan* at the Sita-Ram shrine, Shree Sanatan Mandir, Leicester, UK.

Sita as Shakti

How can you try to understand a worldview if it is different from your own?

---

*S*ita *was really a* shakti, *a goddess. She wasn't just an ordinary woman. She didn't have to act as she did, but she chose to, to help Ram destroy the demons.* Time and again, without being asked, the older women referred to the idea that Sita was a *shakti*. The word means 'power' or 'strength'. A god's *shakti* is his wife or consort. Only through her can he act. This shows us why a *shakti* is thought to be so powerful. It also shows why, for some, rather than being a passive character, Sita is actually the lynch-pin of the whole action.

Sita is a powerful shakti. If she had not existed, the demon [Ravan] would not have acted in the same way. The war would not have taken place to destroy cruelty. Also at the moment of death, Ravan became Ram's devotee. He cried out "Sri Ram" and went to heaven. This was all because Ravan kidnapped Sita. . .The gods can't act without shakti. It's a physical power and a mental inspiration.

Nor is it confined to the gods. At first, I wondered whether the Hindus I interviewed tended to see Sita as more of a human or more of a *shakti*, a goddess. After all, just as Rama is believed to be an **avatar** of Lord Vishnu, so Sita is an avatar of the goddess, **Lakshmi**, Vishnu's wife. Shilpa and Trishna discussed this and came to the conclusion that *she was more a human person with godly ways.* They were struggling to express their feeling that the question was not properly put. Manjusha Acharya put it in a different way. *Yes, I see her as human. But a human figure can have power as well. You can't separate her as a human figure or as a shakti. So many ladies I know now, they did that much* [as much as Sita]. *Men can't do it.*

Left: Kanchan Pankania's shrine, with Sita and Ram. 'The **murtis** are only plastic but I would not change them now. They are too precious to me.'

It is because Sita is seen as a *shakti* that Tina Shah can say:

Don't consider women as the weaker sex any more. Sita is a symbol of great strength. Whenever anything happens, you have to analyse it and live with it amicably. But where wrong is involved, you must stand up against it.

Identifying strongly with Sita's maltreatment by Rama at the end, another wife and mother pointed out:

Sita is also a role model as a shakti. She has hidden power which she uses in the end, when she left Ram suffering. . . She obeyed throughout her life, but in the end she won.

A positive inspiration now? A hope for future relief? Bearing situations or changing them? We go back to a feminist challenge.

To introduce it, we hear a poem, inspired by discussion of Sita's Story, written by one of the interviewees under her pen-name 'Naseev' and translated into English by Maluika Acharya. 'Death' in verse 5 refers not just to actual death but to the mental and physical torture of oppressive relationships. 'Power' in verse 6 is shakti. The original Hindi is at the back of this book.

1) O Lord Rama, during your reign, men had many rights, while women were oppressed and regarded as a toy; that is what they thought.

2) Women were good for companionship during the hard times, but were forgotten during the good.

3) O Sita, at the peril of womanhood, you drove yourself to extremes, just to prove your wifehood.

4) Since these times, men have made many customs — to burn widows in the funeral pyre of their dead husbands.

5) The customs started then are still observed, resulting in the death of numerous innocents.

6) O women of the world, in the name of progress, change history. You are not weak. You are the <u>power</u>. Make sure everyone is aware of it.

Acceptance or Rejection? Domestic Violence and Rape

When and how should we stand up against violence close to home?

Eternal mythologies like the Ramayan are revived and popularised via state controlled media at the mass 'entertainment' level, and the negative values they convey regarding women find more than adequate reflection in textbooks and children's literature at the 'education' level, **say** Kamla Basin and Ritu Menon. With Sita as our ideal, can sati [widow-burning] be far behind? It is this overarching ideology of male superiority and female dispensability that sanctions sati and leads to its glorification, and accepts the silent violence against women that rages in practically every home across the country (quoted in Mark Tully, p.132).

Mark Tully, who quotes this, thinks their last sentence in particular is a huge exaggeration and indeed insult to Indian women. Domestic violence is obviously a very difficult subject and one which we all find hard to talk about, whatever our own background or experience. However, I wondered whether the adults interviewed would have any comments to make on this passage. What emerged was a desire to distinguish quite clearly: the kind of suffering which was not thought to result from injustice; violence and oppression, which was wrong; and the voluntary self-sacrifice of the *sati* (righteous woman) who chooses to give up her life with her husband's. Beyond that there were only hints.

Domestic violence should be answered with violence, said one woman quite uncompromisingly. *Sita is a strong character who stands up to others. It's wrong, though, to say there was violence with Sita. Ram did what was expected of him as king. His love for Sita is made clear, for example, in his pining, but he did what he did for his subjects.*

Sita never went through all that. Ram never beat her up.
She might have, responded a friend. *Nobody knows anybody's personal life. . .*

Violence brings shame. The family is for sorting it. But they wouldn't want to accept this [was happening], said a young man with understanding.

Men always conquer ladies, commented one woman ruefully, describing the fire test Rama put Sita through.

The fire test wasn't, of course, an example of committing 'suttee', that is, where the woman throws herself onto her husband's funeral pyre. Sita is a *sati* in the sense of being a righteous wife, a *pativrata*, one devoted to her husband. She even asks that she may be married to Rama in her next life as she is swallowed up by the earth, but she freely chooses the end of her life and it comes before Rama's own.

The practice of suttee has been illegal in India since 1829, but people continue to have mixed feelings about a woman's right to end her life with her husband's. *I'm totally against forced* sati. *We have got some real satis, pure strong women, who had that power. There's a true story of Jesal and Toral. It's a story from Kutch. Jesal was sati. Toral was a bandit. She was so pure and she changed him. She ended her life with his [not by burning]. They were buried together [as saints]. People started praying to her as a true sati. They say the graves are moving towards each other slowly. There are loads of songs about them.*

Left: Close-up of Sita from a devotional poster.

Sita and Her Story Now

*Why do you think Sita's story remains so important today,
now you have read this book?*

There was no doubt that Sita's story was better known in general to the older generation of Hindus interviewed. It was least well known to two men in their twenties, who thought this might be because the number of Hindus where they live is actually quite small. On the other hand, some of the youngest participants, including one aged nine, had an encyclopaedic grasp of the story, gained from videos, comics and parental explanation. When the younger people themselves marry and have children, it seems likely that many will have the motivation to learn even more of their traditions then.

If I had children, I would pass on the story. It's important if you are living in a society where you are a minority, especially where there are lots of mixed marriages going on. It's part of our heritage, what makes us Hindu. If they don't know these stories, they won't know their cultural identity.

The comments of the Hindus given in this book make it plain that Sita's story continues to be told, watched, questioned and explored, related to life today, as it has been by each generation before us, across India and throughout the world. Sita's appeal remains, as young Hindus go on exploring their identity in the twentieth century, discussing it with parents and siblings, whether in India or abroad. *Perhaps Sita is an example of being faithful to your own identity, even when you are far from home*, mused Shivani Pandey, with an imaginative and powerful interpretation of Sita remaining true to her own traditions, wherever she found herself to be.

If I tried to be a little like that, it'd be alright.
Real people are more important [as examples] *for that*, countered Shilpa.
No, I think stories are, was Trishna's reply.
It's a simple king and queen story, but some of the things in it are very, very deep.

Right: A picture hanging in the Buchechas' shrine room: Hindu values at the heart of the home.

A Last Word on Using the Story

How should we treat what is important to other people, including their stories?

It has been suggested that the story of Rama and Sita is a bit like a mirror. When you hear it or watch it, you can see yourself in it and become almost part of the story, a story told without end. But what do you see when you look?

If you're not Indian or Hindu, you're not really going to know the story or much about Sita. . . It's alright to use her story as long as you don't misrepresent what's being said and don't exploit it, by misrepresenting what it means.

At the end of the day, Rama and Sita is a classical historical story people would like to believe happened and hopefully did, claimed one man. *What's important though is that we take its values forward into the next century. But if you want to bring it down to a feminist analysis of Sita as a role model, you are doing it an injustice. . . Because at that time men and women knew their roles and the divorce rate was minimal. Women would even commit* sati.

That's not good, interrupted the last speaker's sister. *Women would probably rather be living in the modern age.*

But then people are confused about their roles, he responded with some justice.

Or women have opened their eyes a bit, she replied.

So who tells Sita's story now?

Right: A copy of the *Ramcharitmanas,* beautifully wrapped, awaiting its next reading ...

राम तुम्हारे राज्य ने, मर्दों को ये आधिकार दिये,

पत्नि नही खिलौना है, मन में ये क्रूर उदगार भरे ।

सीता तुम वन वन भटकी पत्नि धर्म निभाने को ,

राम ने त्यागा, अग्नि में तपाया, अपनी मर्यादा निभाने को ।

सीता तुमने पत्नित्व का , अस्तित्व ही मिट डाला,

नारीत्व धर्म निभाने को, स्वयं को व्यर्थ जला डाला ।

तव मे मर्दों ने देखो, कैसी प्रथा बना डाली,

जिन्दा स्तियों की यूँ ही, अनगिनत चिता जला डाली ।

राम राज्य मे प्रथा चली तो, अब तक चलती आई है,

ना जाने कितनी मासूमों की हत्या करती आई है ?

जागो, चलो, बढ़ो, प्रगति के पथ पर, कल का इतिहास बदल डाला,

नारी, अबला नही, "शक्ति" है , मर्दों को सबक सिखा डाला ।

नसीव

Glossary

avatar   'descent', especially of Lord Vishnu to earth, in various forms, to restore dharma at times of threat

chopai   one of the Hindi verse forms used in Tulsidas's Ramcharitmanas

darshan   'seeing'; to see/realise the presence of God in the temple image or teacher

Dassehra   tenth night following the nine-night Autumn festival of Navratri; in North India, celebrates Ram's triumph over Ravan

delusion   for many Hindus, the problem of being human is that we do not really know who we are; we are deluded about our own identity, the nature of God and our relation to God. The Ramcharitmanas is believed by many to help us get rid of that delusion.

dharma   order; the order of the whole universe, social order and ritual order; a sense that every human being (and living creature) has its place in a great order of things, whose balance must be maintained, though it declines progressively in each of the great four world ages.

Divali   'row of lights'; festival which falls in late October or November (five days in India). In North India, it celebrates the return of Ram and Sita to Ayodhya, amongst many other things.

gamelan   Javanese orchestra; many of the instruments are a bit like bronze xylophones and are struck with round-ended hammers, making a mellow, haunting sound; others include drums and flutes

Gujarat   state in northwest India, where the language spoken is Gujarati

Hindi	language of much of North India
kirtan	session for singing devotional songs
Maharashtra	state in west India, just south of Gujarat; language spoken is Marathi
murtis	images
Navratri	nine-night festival of worship to the Goddess, held late September or October
puja	worship, especially involving offerings of water, flowers, fruit, lights, offered daily at home shrine by many Hindus
Sanskrit	ancient classical language of India, still used in much ritual today
South Asian	people living in or with backgrounds from Bangladesh, India, Pakistan, Sri Lanka
Tamil	South Indian language, especially spoken in Tamilnadu, a state in southeast India

List of Names and Pronunciation Guide

(aa as in 'car', u as in Southern English 'but')

Ayodhya *(Ay-oh-dhyaa)*

Dashrath's capital, where Ram and Sita rule on their return. The city is now in the north Indian state of Uttar Pradesh. In 1992, the Babri Mosque in Ayodhya was destroyed by Hindus who claimed that the Muslim emperor who built it had pulled down a Hindu temple marking Rama's birthplace to make room for this Muslim place of worship.

Dashrath *(Dush-ruth)*

king of Ayodhya, Ram's father

Hanuman *(Hun-oo-maan)*

devoted monkey deity who serves Ram

Janak/Janaka *(Junuk[a])*

king of Mithila, Sita's father

Janaki *(Junukee)*

Janak's daughter, i.e. Sita

Kaikeyi *(Kai-kay-ee)*

wife of Dashrath, mother of his second son, Bharat

Kaushalya *(Kow-shul-yaa)*

wife of Dashrath, mother of his first son, Ram

Kush *(rhymes with 'push')*

one of Sita's twin sons

Lakshman/Lakshmana *(Lucksh-mun-a)*

faithful half-brother of Ram, twin brother of Shatrughna

Lakshmi *(Lucksh-mee)*

goddess, wife of Lord Vishnu, worshipped at Divali

Lav *(almost like 'love')*

one of Sita's twin sons

Mithila *(Mi-thi-laa)*	Janak's capital, where Sita grew up
Parvati *(Paar-vut-ee)*	goddess, wife of Lord Shiv (see another book in this series)
Ram/Rama *(Raam/Raama)*	Hindi and Sanskrit forms of name of the hero of the story, believed by many to be an **avatar** of Lord Vishnu or earthly form of Ultimate Reality
Rama *(Raa-maa)*	another name for Sita (=Rama's wife)
Ramayana/Ramayan *(Raa-maa-yuna)*	title of Valmiki's poem, often used for story itself
Ravan/Ravana *(Raa-vuna)*	name of the anti-hero of the story, demon-king of Lanka
Shatrughna *(Shut-rugh-na)*	twin brother of Lakshman
Shiv/Shiva *(Shiv/Shiver)*	Hindi and Sanskrit forms of names of great god, Lord Shiv; for many Hindus, Lord Shiv is Ultimate Reality, other gods just forms of him
Shurpanakha *(Shur-punukha)*	sister of Ravan
Sita *(See-taa)*	heroine, Ram's wife, seen by many as a form of goddess Lakshmi; shadow Sita or 'pretend' Sita captured by Ravan, after Ram hid real Sita in the first fire
Urmila *(Oor-mee-laa)*	Lakshman's wife
Vishnu *(Vish-noo)*	great god, Lord Vishnu; for some Hindus, Lord Vishnu is Ultimate Reality, the other gods just forms of him. Tulsidas sees the Name (of Ram) as Ultimate Reality and other gods as forms

Versions of Sita's Story Referred to in this Book

(those mentioned most frequently are in **bold***; sources are given in approximate chronological order)*

AUTHOR	TITLE AND DETAILS
Valmiki	**Ramayana** (literally, **'The going or path of Rama'**, Rama being amongst us) written in Sanskrit in 7 books, core goes back at least to 5th century BCE
Kamban	*Iramavataram,* maybe 12th century CE, in Tamil (South Indian language)
anon.	*Adhyatma-ramayana* ('Ramayana of the inner self'), Sanskrit, probably late 15th or early 16th century CE, Advaitin (i.e. takes view that the self, stripped of the individuality of mind-body, and ultimate reality are identical)
Atukuri Molla	*Molla Ramayanam* written in Telegu, early 16th c. CE, by a woman poet, one of the versions which stresses Sita's childhood and coming of age
Tulsidas	**Ramcharitmanas ('Lake of the Exploits of Ram')**, 16th c. CE Hindi, still very popular and translated into other modern Indian languages, including Gujarati
Rampriya Sharan	*Sitayan* c.1703, in Hindi, in 7 books, just on Sita's childhood and marriage (To help his devotion to Sita-Ram, the author thought of himself as one of Sita's sisters)
King Rama I	commissioned the Ramakien Thai version of 1797, based on older Thai and Indian versions

women's songs	written in the Telugu language, from Andhra Pradesh, state in east India; and in Gujarati and Marathi languages, from Gujarat and Maharashtra, states in west India
Morari Bapu	*Mangal Ramayan* 1980s English version (also in Gujarati) with his explanations

Ramanand Sagar Doordarshan (Indian TV) 1987-88 version: based largely on Tulsidas, though Ramanand claims to have consulted widely. The credits mention traditions in Tamil, Marathi, Telugu, Bengali, Kannada, Malayalam, Urdu and Hindi (major languages of modern India). This is to suggest the universality of the TV version, against possible criticisms that it favours Hindi. I am grateful to Dr John Brockington for this information.

SITA'S STORY: OTHER BOOKS QUOTED OR REFERRED TO:

Kakar, Sudhir 'Feminine Identity in India' in Rehana Ghadially, *Women in Indian Society* London, Sage, 1988 (referred to in 'Sita's qualities')

Lutgendorf, Philip *The Life of a Text: Performing the* Ramcaritmanas *of Tulsidas* Berkeley: University of California Press, 1991 (quoted in 'Why go on telling the story?')

Poitevin, Guy and Hema Rairkar *Indian Peasant Women Speak up*, translated by Michel Leray, Bombay: Orient Longman, ET 1993 (quoted in 'The ideal wife, family member and mother')

Shulman, David 'Fire and Flood: the testing of Sita in Kampan's *Iramavataram,* in Paula Richman (ed) *Many Ramayanas: the diversity of a narrative tradition in South Asia,* Berkeley: University of California Press, 1991 (quoted in 'Sita: weak or strong?')

Tully, Mark *No Full Stops in India* Harmondsworth: Penguin, 1992 (quoted in 'Acceptance or Rejection? Domestic violence and rape')

Tulsidas *Sri Ramacharitamanasa with Hindi text and English translation* Gorakhpur: Gita Press, n.d. (quoted in 'Sita's story')

A Note for Teachers

This book has been tried out with pupils of varying abilities aged from 13 to 18, in Personal and Social Education classes, general Religious Education and examination level (GCSE and 'A' level) Religious Studies groups.

Possible course units: on Hindu traditions, introduced through a core story, its related festivals and values; on religious myths and the ways in which they help human beings structure everyday life and their understanding of the Ultimate; on family values in different traditions; on domestic violence and rape; on diversity within religious traditions, for example, in attitudes to women. In each case, the story should be carefully and appropriately introduced, so that pupils have a context in which to work. A key point to draw out would be the great variety of ways in which Hindus, as others, approach the resources of their own traditions.

Suggestions for use:
1) Teacher reads or tells story (pp. 13–22). Pupils compare with the way the story is told in Westhill Divali filmstrip or Amar Chitra Katha comic or summary in any other textbook. Why the differences? Look at devotional pictures, for example, of Sita's kidnap, crowning of Rama and Sita. Produce, for example, own comic strip, shadow puppet play, video of puppets, after discussion, for specified audience (for example, younger pupils, parents who do not know anything about Hindu traditions, etc., to help them 'get inside' the story).

2) Start with one of the discussion questions. For example, what expectations do you have of your family and your family of you (p.35). Get one or two suggestions, then pupils work in groups brainstorming. Discuss. Where do these expectations come from? Are they reasonable? What can you do when you disagree? With book, in pairs, what expectations did the interviewees identify? What different attitudes did they have towards these expectations? Feedback in whole group. How can we learn to understand others whose expectations and attitudes are different from our own?

3) Pupils in pairs take a section of the book each. From that section, what sort of person does Sita seem to be? What qualities does she have? Do you see these as positive or negative qualities? Or, as ambiguous ones? Does it depend on the circumstances? What makes the difference? Individuals write a magazine feature article on Sita. Display and compare different versions.

4) In whole group, read and discuss poems/songs based on story. How do they help the people who read/sing them to come to terms with their own circumstances? Do they accept the story without question? How can poems and stories help us to question, resist, channel, upset, understand? Pupils take an incident/issue in the story and write a poem reflecting their own attitude to similar circumstances in their own lives or attitude of one of the people interviewed.

5) At the end of the book, one man interviewed observes: "People are confused about their roles [i.e. nowadays]." "Or women have opened their eyes a bit," his sister replies. One half of the class uses book to find examples of statements about roles. Other half looks for evidence of women questioning or reinterpreting traditional roles. In discussion: what roles do people play in their own families? Do they want to play the same roles as their parents? Why/not? What are advantages and disadvantages of being a 'liberated' woman or man?

6) How are values passed down? What do the pupils think are the most effective ways? Foe example, stories, rules, personal example, life stories of others? What do the people in the book think? Why don't the women on p.33 say to their daughters, "Be like Sita"? Do the pupils think this is wise? Can they think of any examples of stories they have heard, biographical or fictional, where they have thought, "O yes, life is like that"?

Acknowledgements

We are grateful to the following for permission to reproduce photographs and other copyright material: Chris Nicol (p.8); Amar Chitra Katha, 1994, India Book House Ltd (p.19); British Museum Trustees (p.6); Mrs Kanchan Pankhania (p.24); K Printers, Wembley (p.27); Bharat Kala Bhavan, Banaras Hindu University (p.32) Kaushik, Edgware (p.36); Ram Mandir, Leicester (p.47); pages 11, 12, 14, 20, 23, 28, 41, 44, 48, 55, 57, by Jacqueline Suthren Hirst

Best efforts were made to obtain permission to reprint: National Museum, New Delhi (p.16).

Fiona Whitchelo first drew my attention to the article by Sudhir Kakar. I would like to thank the following for reading parts of the book and offering helpful comments, though I must take responsibility for its final form: Chris Nicol and pupils from Chesterton Community College, Cambridge, UK; Andrew Priory and pupils from The King's School, Chester, UK; Sarah Priory and pupils from Upton-by-Chester County High School, Chester, UK. In particular, I thank Dr John Brockington of the Department of Sanskrit, University of Edinburgh, Scotland, UK, for his careful reading and suggestions.